Bible Activity Sheets
for Special Days

Bible Activity Sheets for Special Days

Betty De Vries
and
Mary F. Loeks

BAKER BOOK HOUSE

Grand Rapids, Michigan 49516

Copyright 1987 by
Baker Book House Company

ISBN: 0-8010-2971-6

Fifth printing, November 1991

Printed in the United States of America

Puzzles 49-88 were taken from *Christmas Activity Book* by Mary F. Loeks, Dwight Baker, illustrator, copyright 1979 by Baker Book House Company, and *Christmas Cut-n-Color Book* by Betty De Vries, Jan Ensing Keelean and Walter Kerr, illustrator, copyright 1983 by Baker Book House Company. Other illustrations were drawn by Cheryl Strikwerda Randall.

Contents

Jesus' Life

1. MAP

This is a map of Judah, Samaria, and Galilee at the time Jesus was on earth. The lines show some of the trips he made when He was young. Color the countries in yellow and orange. Color the seas blue.

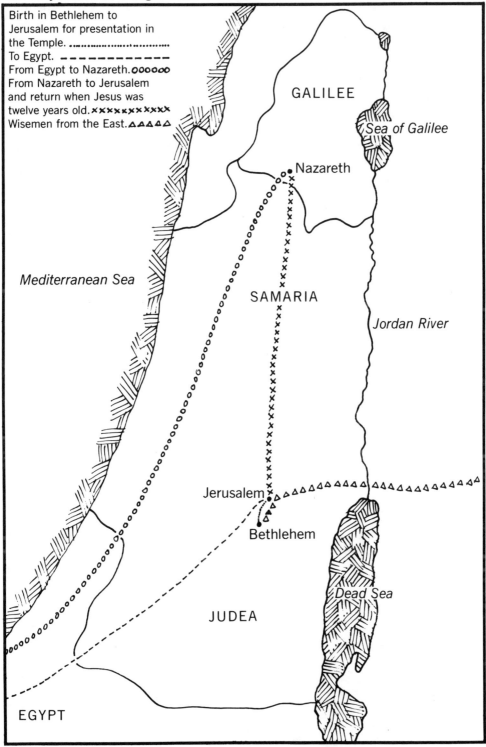

Birth in Bethlehem to
Jerusalem for presentation in
the Temple. ....
To Egypt. – – – – – – – –
From Egypt to Nazareth. oooooo
From Nazareth to Jerusalem
and return when Jesus was
twelve years old. xxxxxxxxxx
Wisemen from the East. △△△△△

GALILEE

Sea of Galilee

• Nazareth

Mediterranean Sea

SAMARIA

Jordan River

Jerusalem

Bethlehem

Dead Sea

JUDEA

EGYPT

2. THEY KNEW JESUS

Jesus had many friends. Some of the friends had the same name. Joseph was the name of Jesus' earthly father. Joseph of Arimathea gave a tomb so that there would be a place where Jesus could be buried. See if you can name more friends (or enemies) with the same name and then unscramble the names on the next page.

Draw a line from column one to the matching name in column two.

COLUMN ONE

1 Beggar outside the gate (Luke 16:20)

2 Betrayer (Luke 22:48)

3 King when Jesus was born (Matt. 2:1)

4 Another name for Peter (Matt. 4:18)

5 Brother of the disciple James (Matt. 10:2)

6 Mother of Jesus (Luke 2:5-7)

COLUMN TWO

1 Friend who Jesus raised from the dead (John 12:17)

2 Forerunner of Jesus (Luke 1:36, 57-60)

3 Sister of Lazarus (John 11:2)

4 Brother of Jesus (Matt. 13:55)

5 He bore Jesus' cross (Matt. 27:32)

6 King who ordered John the Baptist to be killed (Matt. 14:6-10)

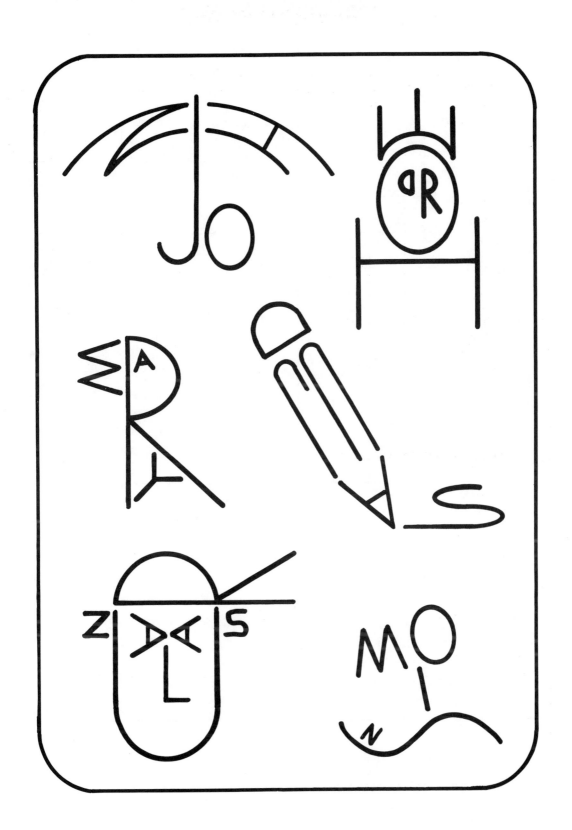

3. GOOD SHEPHERD STACK-A-WORD

Clues

The verses below are taken from John 10:1–15 (NIV). The words which have been left out are the ones you need to fill in the crossword on the previous page. A = across, D = down.

". . . the man who does not enter the __6 D__ __15 A__ by the __11 D__, but climbs in by some other way, is a thief and a __12 A__. The man who enters by the __11 D__ is the __7 A__ . . . . He __9 A__ his __5 A__ __6 D__ by __14 A__ and leads them out . . . his __6 D__ __2 A__ him because they __4 D__ his __1 D__. But they will never __2 A__ a stranger; in fact, they will __13 D__ away from him. . . ." Jesus said again, "I tell you the truth, I am the __11 D__ for the __6 D__ . . . whoever enters through me will be saved. He will come in and go out, and find __8 D__ . . . . I have come that they may have __10 D__, and have it to the full. I am the good __7 A__. The good __7 A__ lays down his __10 D__ for the __6 D__ . . . . When [the hired hand] sees the __3 D__ coming, he abandons the __6 D__ and runs away. . . . I am the good __7 A__; I __4 D__ my __6 D__ and my __6 D__ __4 D__ me . . . I lay down my __10 D__ for the __6 D__."

Can you write the name of one of Jesus' sheep?

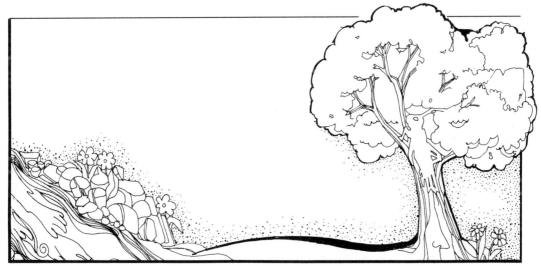

13

4. SMOKE SIGNALS

Can you read Joel's message? Follow the white smoke all the way up to a letter and then write the letter in one of the squares above the smoke.

5. FIND THE SHEEP

There are thirteen sheep hiding in the picture below. How many sheep can you find?

6. JESUS' WORDS

In John 10 Jesus tried to tell his friends what he was going to do. Change the numbers below to the corresponding letter to find out what Jesus said.

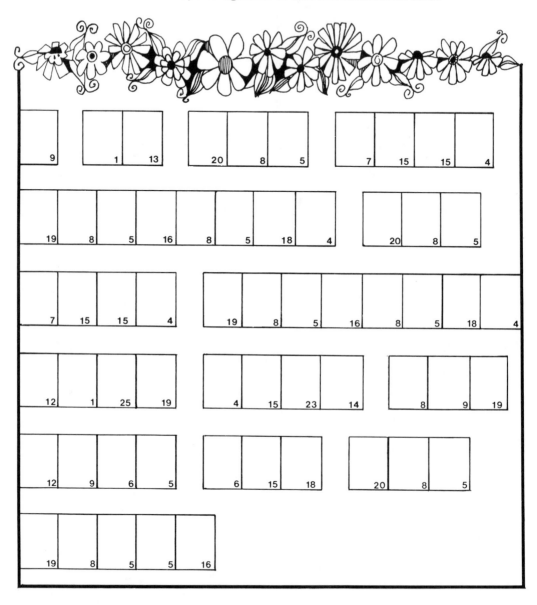

Valentine's Day

7. HEART PUZZLE

Here's a heart puzzle for you to color, cut out, and put back together.

8. JESUS LOVES CHILDREN

Can you find the word JESUS, 6 hearts, 3 girls, and 3 boys hidden in the picture below?

9. SMOKE SIGNALS

Can you read Joel's message? Follow the white smoke all the way up to a letter and then write the letter in one of the squares above the smoke.

10. SIX LOVE MESSAGES

These are love messages found in the Bible. To discover what they are, put one letter from the columns below into each square. A black square means the end of a word.

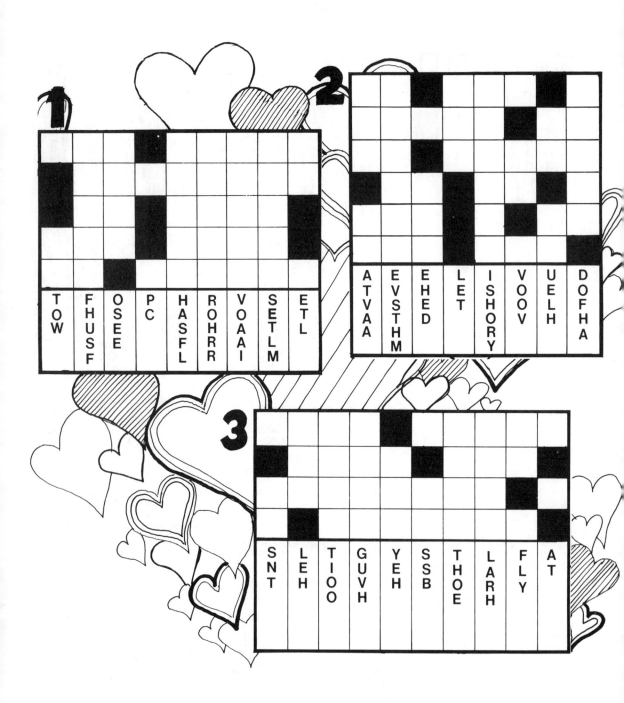

1

T O W	F H U S F	O S E E	P C	H A S F L	R O H R R	V O A A I	S E T L M	E T L

2

A T V A A	E V S T H M	E H E D	L E T	I S H O R Y	V O O V	U E L H	D O F H A

3

S N T	L E H	T I O O	G U V H	Y E H	S S B	T H O E	L A R H	F L Y	A T

4

EAHPI	NAFS	TODOH	TRIMF	SHEW	GTEEN	CHOT	ISLOKO	SOME	VETM

5

STO	LAI	FWONAL	OOLEV	GETSV	OHEOO	DODUE	RGNT	SUEOH

6

DOIK	EEVCM	OEEE	NMPY	MEMT	MASE	YNL

Easter

11. SOME EASTER FACTS

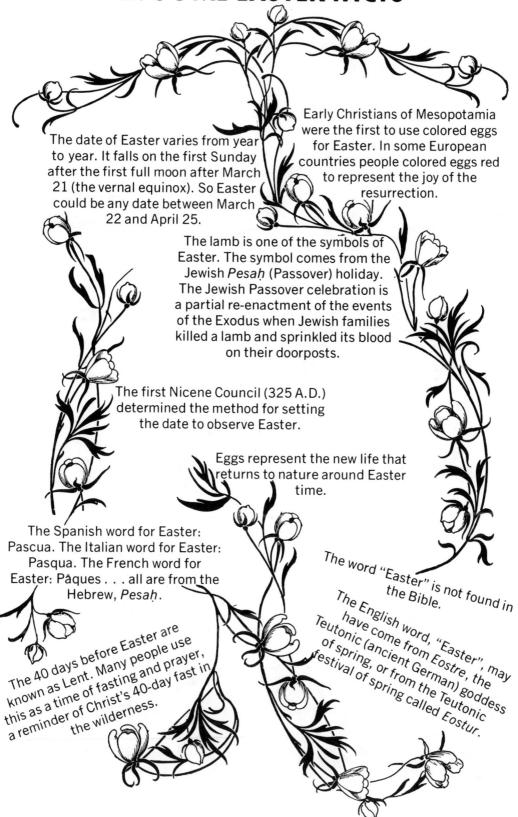

The date of Easter varies from year to year. It falls on the first Sunday after the first full moon after March 21 (the vernal equinox). So Easter could be any date between March 22 and April 25.

Early Christians of Mesopotamia were the first to use colored eggs for Easter. In some European countries people colored eggs red to represent the joy of the resurrection.

The lamb is one of the symbols of Easter. The symbol comes from the Jewish *Pesah* (Passover) holiday. The Jewish Passover celebration is a partial re-enactment of the events of the Exodus when Jewish families killed a lamb and sprinkled its blood on their doorposts.

The first Nicene Council (325 A.D.) determined the method for setting the date to observe Easter.

Eggs represent the new life that returns to nature around Easter time.

The Spanish word for Easter: Pascua. The Italian word for Easter: Pasqua. The French word for Easter: Pâques . . . all are from the Hebrew, *Pesah*.

The word "Easter" is not found in the Bible. The English word, "Easter", may have come from Eostre, the Teutonic (ancient German) goddess of spring, or from the Teutonic festival of spring called Eostur.

The 40 days before Easter are known as Lent. Many people use this as a time of fasting and prayer, a reminder of Christ's 40-day fast in the wilderness.

12. WHY?

Jesus told Pilate, "You would have no power over me if it were not given to you from above." Why was Jesus willing to die on the cross?

To find out the answer, cross out all D's, F's, G's, I's, J's, K's, N's, P's, Q's, R's, T's, W's, X's, Y's, and Z's.

D B I E Q C I A U S I E

I H N P E W Q Z Y J G X

G L D F O V I J E K S N

M D Q I K N R T E Y P I

13. EASTER MESSAGE

Color in those spaces of the puzzle below which have dots in them. Discover Easter's most important message.

14. WORD CHALLENGE

Can you make at least 50 words from the letters in
"JESUS HAS RISEN"?

_____   _____   _____   _____

_____   _____   _____   _____

_____   _____   _____   _____

_____   _____   _____   _____

_____   _____   _____   _____

_____   _____   _____   _____

_____   _____   _____   _____

_____   _____   _____   _____

_____   _____   _____   _____

_____   _____   _____   _____

_____   _____   _____   _____

_____   _____   _____   _____

_____   _____   _____   _____

_____   _____   _____   _____

_____   _____   _____   _____

_____   _____   _____   _____

_____   _____   _____   _____

15. EASTER WORD HUNT

The angel's words (Matt. 28:5–7) have been hidden in this word square. Look up, down, sideways, backwards and diagonally to find the words. If a word appears more than once in the verses, it is hidden only once in the square.

THE ANGEL SAID TO THE WOMEN, "DO NOT BE AFRAID, FOR I KNOW THAT YOU ARE LOOKING FOR JESUS, WHO WAS CRUCIFIED. HE IS NOT HERE; HE HAS RISEN, JUST AS HE SAID. COME AND SEE THE PLACE WHERE HE LAY. THEN GO QUICKLY AND TELL HIS DISCIPLES: 'HE HAS RISEN FROM THE DEAD' . . ."

```
M R A S S E L P I C S I D
E R E H W Y L K C I U Q T
E M O C L T G D N A J E E
C S L O S A O E N E U E L
A B C Q A H S N S A S L L
L K N O W I A U I M T O D
P A F O R S S L O H L I N
C B M S L A Z R E Q A E B
A E M N I C F N O S Y R E
N U N D L H E R A O D E C
G Y O U S L T H A T A H A
E H T C R U C I F I E D L
L O O K I N G N A M D O Q
```

16. RESURRECTION STACK-A-WORD

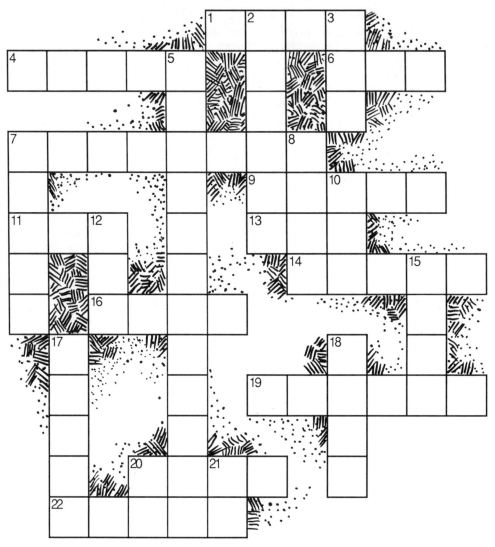

Clues

Fill in the blanks with the word that best fits the verse. Then complete the puzzle on the next page with the words that completed the clue.

Clues Across

1. _____ went to the tomb. (John 20:1)

4. _____ and another disciple started for the tomb. (John 20:3)

6. There is but _____ true God.

7. Just before he died, Jesus said, "It is _____". (John 19:30)

9. Only strips of _____ were in the tomb. (John 20:6)

11. The disciples _____ to the tomb. (John 20:4)

13. Jesus told Thomas to _____ his hands. (John 20:27)

14. An old word which means live. "I will _____ in the house of the Lord forever." (Psalm 23:6)

16. Mary was _____ing because her friend Jesus had died. (The word means to cry.)

19. Two friends of Jesus wrapped his body with the _____, in strips of linen. (John 19:40)

20. Mary went here, early on Easter morning. (John 20:1)

22. She saw that the _____ had been removed from the entrance. (John 20:1)

Clues Down

2. (#1) saw two _____ dressed in white. (John 20:12)

3. "These are written that _____ may believe." (John 20:31)

5. Jesus said, "I am the _____ and the life." (John 11:25)

7. Jesus rose on the _____ day of the week. (John 20:1)

8. Jesus _____ on the cross for you and me.

10. Jesus was put in a _____ tomb. (John 19:41, 42)

12. Jesus said, "A _____ command I give you: Love one another." (John 13:34)

15. By believing you may have _____ in his name." (John 20:31)

17. Mary thought he was the gardener. (John 20:15–16)

18. The risen Jesus cooked a breakfast of _____ for his disciples. (John 21:12–13)

20. While it was still dark, Mary went _____ the tomb. (John 20:1)

21. Jesus said, "Remember _____."

17. WHICH ARE EASTER PICTURES?

Color each of the pictures on these pages. Which shows an important part of, or reason for, the events of Easter?

18. FOLLOW THE EASTER STORY

On the next four pages you will find twelve pictures and descriptions of events that took place a few days before and just after Jesus was crucified. Put these pictures in the order in which the events took place. Place the letter you find with each picture in the correctly numbered box below. Example: The picture of the first event is *Jesus is betrayed*. That picture has an "R" with it, so put an "R" in the box numbered 1.

If you have finished correctly, you will have spelled out something which happened to Jesus that is the most important event in all of history.

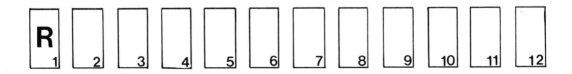

R											
1	2	3	4	5	6	7	8	9	10	11	12

Jesus is betrayed.
Luke 22:47, 48

Two criminals are put on crosses
beside Jesus.
Luke 23:32–33

N

Jesus cooks a breakfast of fish and
bread for his disciples.
John 21:4–13

E

Pilate orders Jesus' execution, then
washes his hands of it.
Matt. 27:24, 26

E

Jesus is sent before Caiaphas, the
high priest.
John 18:24

R

Barabbas is released.
Luke 23:18, 25

Jesus said, "Father, forgive them,
for they do not know what they are
doing."
Luke 23:34

Peter denies Jesus the third time.
Luke 22:60, 61

The risen Jesus appears to Mary.
John 20:13–18

Herod and his soldiers mock Jesus.
Luke 23:11

Jesus is brought before Pilate
(first time).
Luke 23:1

Simon of Cyrene is ordered to carry
Jesus' cross.
Luke 23:26

19. THE EMPTY TOMB

Help Peter and John find Jesus' empty tomb.

20. GOD'S EASTER GIFT

What is God's Easter gift to us? Can you read the message? If you need a clue, turn this page upside down.

HQT IQF UQ NQXGF VJG
YQTNF VJCV JG ICXG JKU
QPG CPF QPNA UQP, VJCV
YJQGXGT DGNKGXGU KP JKO UJCNN
PQV RGTKUJ DWV JCXG GVGTPCN
NKHG.

Take each letter and go back two letters in the alphabet.

21. WHO AM I?

Give yourself five points if you can guess correctly with only the first clue; three points if you can guess on the second clue; and one point if you can guess after the third clue.

1. My appearance was like lightning.

   My clothes were white as snow.

   I rolled the stone away from the entrance to Jesus' tomb and sat on it.

   Who am I? _____ Points: _____

2. I am a rich man from Arimathea.

   I am a follower of Jesus.

   Jesus was placed in the unused cave, which was to be my tomb.

   Who am I? _____ Points: _____

3. We were Pilate's soldiers.

   We were sent on a spooky assignment.

   Something happened that so frightened us that we shook and became like dead men.

   Who were we? _____ Points: _____

4. We followed Jesus from Galilee to care for his needs.

   From a distance, we watched Jesus die.

   Early on Easter morning, we brought spices to Jesus' tomb to preserve his body.

   Who were we? _____ Points: _____

5. It was my job to watch Jesus die.

   I felt the earthquake, saw rocks split, and saw dead people come alive when Jesus died.

   I said, "Surely he was the Son of God!"

   Who am I? _____ Points: _____

22. SOME EASTER PEOPLE

The drawings below are made from the letters in the names of some people we read about in the Bible's Easter story.

23. CHANGE-A-LETTER

What can God's child say, because of what happened at Easter time?
Change one letter in each of the words below.

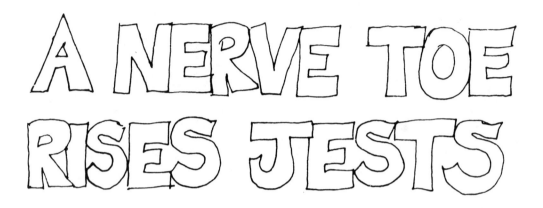

A NERVE TOE
RISES JESTS

24. TRUE OR FALSE?

If the statement is *true*, circle the letter in the True column. If the statement is *false*, circle the letter in the False column.

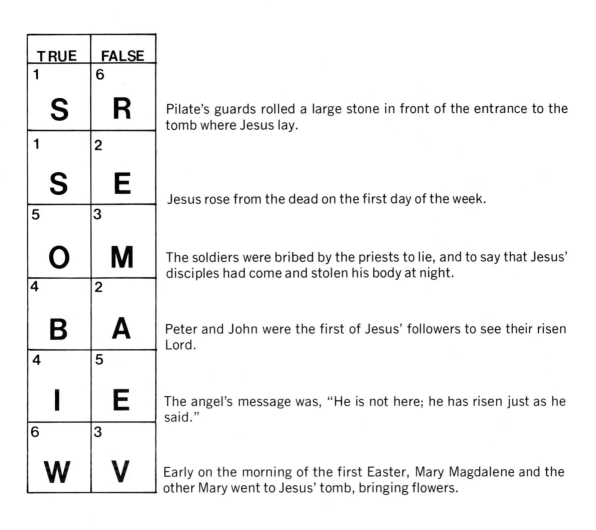

TRUE	FALSE	
1 **S**	6 **R**	Pilate's guards rolled a large stone in front of the entrance to the tomb where Jesus lay.
1 **S**	2 **E**	Jesus rose from the dead on the first day of the week.
5 **O**	3 **M**	The soldiers were bribed by the priests to lie, and to say that Jesus' disciples had come and stolen his body at night.
4 **B**	2 **A**	Peter and John were the first of Jesus' followers to see their risen Lord.
4 **I**	5 **E**	The angel's message was, "He is not here; he has risen just as he said."
6 **W**	3 **V**	Early on the morning of the first Easter, Mary Magdalene and the other Mary went to Jesus' tomb, bringing flowers.

Now put the letters you circled in the squares below, matching the number of the square with the number beside the letter.

"For unto you is born this day a

1	2	3	4	5	6

The fact that Jesus died and rose again fulfills this promise that the angels made at the time of Jesus' birth.

45

25. EASTER V.I.P. STACK-A-WORD

Across

3. The Roman governor who gave the order for Jesus to be crucified. Luke 23:23–25

5. This man placed Jesus' body in his own, unused tomb. Luke 23:50-53

6. Once he visited Jesus by night. He provided myrrh and aloes and helped prepare Jesus' body for burial. John 19:39

7. He was the Jewish high priest who later sent Jesus to Pilate. John 18:24

10. Two women by this name went early Easter morning to the tomb. Matt. 28:1

Down

1. The angels told the women to "Go tell his disciples and _____" that Jesus had indeed risen from the dead. Mark 16:7

2. This man from Cyrene was asked to carry Jesus' cross. Luke 23:26

4. This disciple, being younger and faster, reached the tomb first. (He also wrote this book of the Bible). John 20:3, 4

5. The angel said to the women, "Do not be afraid, for I know that you are looking for _____ who was crucified . . . ." Matt. 28:5

8. He was the one who rolled back the stone from the entrance to the tomb. Matt. 28:2

9. The Roman governor tried to send Jesus back to this man, who was the Jewish ruler of Galilee, appointed by the Romans. Luke 23:6–7

26. WHO SAID IT?

1. "My kingdom is not of this world." John 18:36

2. "Don't have anything to do with that innocent man, for I have suffered a great deal today in a dream because of him." Matt. 27:19

3. "Friend, do what you came for." Matt. 26:50

4. "I don't know the man." Matt. 26:72

5. "What is truth?" John 18:38

6. "I have sinned . . . for I have betrayed innocent blood." Matt. 27:4

7. "Before the rooster crows, you will disown me three times." Matt. 26:75

8. "Are you not going to answer? What is this testimony that these men are bringing against you?" Matt. 26:62

9. "Take him away! Crucify him!" John 19:12, 15

10. "Surely he was the Son of God!" Matt. 27:54

11. "I am thirsty." John 19:28

12. "Mary." John 20:16

13. "I have seen the Lord!" John 20:18

14. "But go, tell his disciples and Peter, 'He is going ahead of you into Galilee. There you will see him, just as he told you.'" Mark 16:7

BIBLE SUNDAY

27. PICTURE MESSAGE

To read this message, take the first letter of the names of these objects and read from left to right.

28. A WALL OF LETTERS

To unscramble the message in this wall of letters, use only the letters in the odd-numbered columns the first time through. On the second try, use only the letters in the even-numbered squares. Write the message on the lines below.

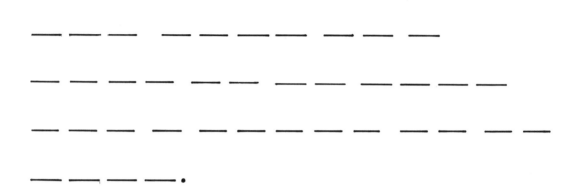

___ ___ ___ ___ ___ ___ ___ ___ ___

___ ___ ___ ___ ___ ___ ___

___ ___ ___ ___ ___ ___ ___ ___ ___

___ ___ ___ ___ .

1	2	3	4	5	6	7	8	9	10	11	12	13
T	T	H	A	Y	N	W	D	O	A	R	L	D
I	I	S	G	A	H	L	T	A	T	M	O	P
T	M	O	Y	M	P	Y	A	F	T	E	H	E

ASCENSION DAY

29. ASCENSION WORD FIND

How many new words can you make from the letters in

ASCENDED! ALLELUIA!

Score 1 point for each letter in the word. For example, *candles* would count 7 points. Can you score 100 points?

_____   _____   _____   _____

_____   _____   _____   _____

_____   _____   _____   _____

_____   _____   _____   _____

_____   _____   _____   _____

_____   _____   _____   _____

_____   _____   _____   _____

_____   _____   _____   _____

_____   _____   _____   _____

_____   _____   _____   _____

_____   _____   _____   _____

_____   _____   _____   _____

_____   _____   _____   _____

_____   _____   _____   _____

_____   _____   _____   _____

_____   _____   _____   _____

_____   _____   _____   _____

_____   _____   _____   _____

30. CHRIST ASCENDING

A cloud received him out of their sight. Acts 1:9

Cut out the two shapes and paste the tabs in the squares indicated. Then pull apart cotton balls and paste bits on the cloud shapes.

Fold on dotted line.

Fold on dotted line.

31. CROWNS AND HARPS

Golden harps are sounding,
Angel voices sing,
Heaven's gates are opened,
Opened for the King.
Jesus, King of Glory,
Jesus, King of Love,
Is gone up in triumph
To his throne above.

Frances R. Havergal, 1871

There are ten harps and twelve crowns hidden in the drawing. How many can you find?

PENTECOST

32. WORD SEARCH

Pentecost is the birthday of the church. Read about it in Acts 2. People from seventeen cities or countries heard the disciples speak in each of their native languages. The names of those countries and/or people are hidden in the puzzle below.

```
A I M A T O P O S E M
I I D C R E T A N S A
C E L C J U D E A R P
O L I Y J E A A I S A
D A B R H P R I H G Y
A M Y E G P O N T U S
P I A N L I M P R T E
P T B E M O R A A P D
A E A I G Y R H P Y E
C S N A E L I L A G M
E L S B A R A L G E P
```

MEDES	CRETANS	PARTHIANS
EGYPT	ELAMITES	GALILEANS
JUDEA	PONTUS	PAMPHYLIA
LIBYA	CYRENE	MESOPOTAMIA
ARABS	ASIA	CAPPADOCIA
PHRYGIA	ROME	

33. PENTECOST MOBILE

Two symbols for the Holy Spirit who was given to Christians on Pentecost, are the dove and tongues of fire. Color the symbols on these pages, then cut them out and make a mobile. Glue the front and back of each dove together and punch out a small hole on top and put a piece of string through each. Put a knot at the end so that the string cannot slip through the hole. Do the same with the tongues of fire. Bend a lightweight coat hanger and hang the doves and the tongues of fire from it.

34. CIRCLE MESSAGE

Something wonderful happened to the disciples on Pentecost. To discover what it was, start at the letter T and the arrow. Then skip every other letter in two trips around the circle. Also skip over the starter T when you begin your second trip around the circle. Print the letters on the blanks inside the circle. The last letter will end on the T where you started.

TRINITY SUNDAY

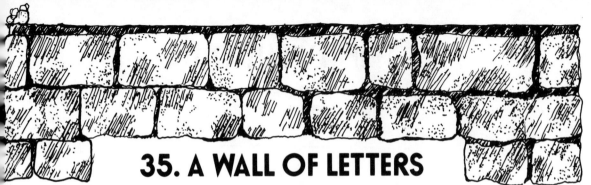

35. A WALL OF LETTERS

To unscramble the message in this wall of letters, use only the letters in the odd-numbered columns the first time through. On the second try, use only the letters in the even-numbered squares. Write the message on the lines below the wall.

___ _____ __ ____

___ ____ __ ___ ____

___ ____ ____ ____

___ ___ _____ ____

__ ____ ___ ____ ____

__ ____ ___ .

1	2	3	4	5	6	7	8	9	10
T	A	H	N	E	D	G	T	R	H
A	E	C	F	E	E	O	L	F	L
T	O	H	W	E	S	L	H	O	I
R	P	D	O	J	F	E	T	S	H
U	E	S	H	C	O	H	L	R	Y
I	S	S	P	T	I	A	R	N	I
D	T	T	B	H	E	E	W	L	I
O	T	V	H	E	Y	O	O	F	U
G	A	O	L	D	L				

36. TRINITY CUT OUTS

Color and cut out these symbols for the Father, the Son, and the Holy Spirit—the Holy Trinity, one God in three distinct and equal persons.

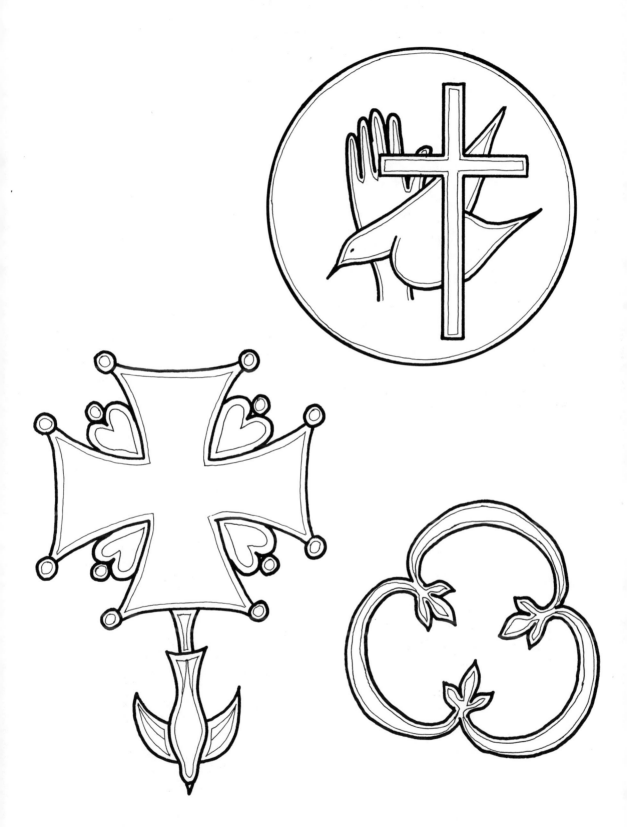

MOTHER'S DAY

37. A FAMOUS MOTHER

Color the spaces marked with a dot to discover the name of a famous mother.

38. A BOOKMARK FOR MOTHER

Carefully color both front and back of the bookmark. Cut out the pieces and paste them together for a special bookmark for your mother.

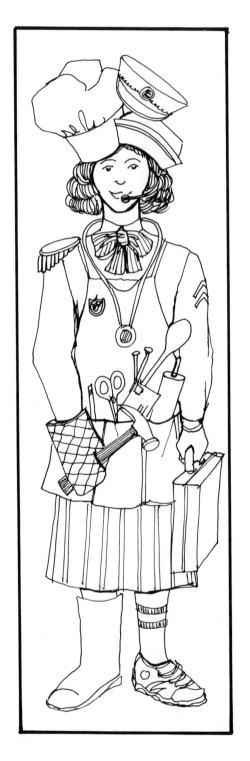

39. MOTHER'S DAY CODED MESSAGE

See if you can decode this special message for Mom, using the key at the bottom of the page.

$\overline{11}\ \overline{2}\ \overline{19}\quad \overline{7}\ \overline{11}\ \overline{3}\ \overline{14}\ \overline{8}\ \overline{19}\ \overline{2}\ \overline{16}\quad \overline{1}\ \overline{19}\ \overline{3}\ \overline{20}\ \overline{2}$

$\overline{5}\ \overline{17}{}'\ \overline{1}\ \overline{12}\ \overline{8}\quad \overline{7}\ \overline{1}\ \overline{14}\ \overline{14}\quad \overline{11}\ \overline{2}\ \overline{19}$

$\overline{6}\ \overline{14}\ \overline{2}\ \overline{20}\ \overline{20}\ \overline{2}\ \overline{8}{}';\quad \overline{11}\ \overline{2}\ \overline{19}\quad \overline{11}\ \overline{5}\ \overline{20}\ \overline{6}\ \overline{1}\ \overline{16}\ \overline{8}$

$\overline{1}\ \overline{14}\ \overline{20}\ \overline{4}{}',\ \overline{1}\ \overline{16}\ \overline{8}\quad \overline{11}\ \overline{2}\quad \overline{17}\ \overline{19}\ \overline{1}\ \overline{3}\ \overline{20}\ \overline{2}\ \overline{21}\ \overline{11}$

31:28

$\overline{11}\ \overline{2}\ \overline{19}.\quad \overline{17}\ \overline{19}\ \overline{4}\ \overline{22}\ \overline{2}\ \overline{19}\ \overline{6}\ \overline{20}$

THE KEY:

1	2	3	4	5	6	7	8	9	10	11	12	13	14	15	16	17	18	19
A	E	I	O	U	B	C	D	F	G	H	J	K	L	M	N	P	Q	R

20	21	22	23	24
S	T	V	W	Y

FATHER'S DAY

40. THE FIRST FATHER

Color the spaces marked with a dot to discover the name of the first father.

41. A BOOKMARK FOR FATHER

Carefully color both front and back of the bookmark. Cut out the pieces and paste them together for a special bookmark for your father.

42. FATHER'S DAY CODED MESSAGE

See if you can decode this message about obedience, using the key at the bottom of this page.

$\overline{11}$ $\overline{2}$ $\overline{1}$ $\overline{19}$ $\overline{21}$ $\overline{11}$ $\overline{2}$

$\overline{3}$ $\overline{16}$ $\overline{20}$ $\overline{21}$ $\overline{19}$ $\overline{5}$ $\overline{7}$ $\overline{21}$ $\overline{3}$ $\overline{4}$ $\overline{16}$ $\overline{4}$ $\overline{9}$ $\overline{21}$ $\overline{11}$ $\overline{24}$

$\overline{9}$ $\overline{1}$ $\overline{21}$ $\overline{11}$ $\overline{2}$ $\overline{19}$ $\overline{17}$ $\overline{19}$ $\overline{4}$ $\overline{22}$ $\overline{2}$ $\overline{19}$ $\overline{6}$ $\overline{20}$ 1:8

THE KEY:

$\frac{1}{A}$	$\frac{2}{E}$	$\frac{3}{I}$	$\frac{4}{O}$	$\frac{5}{U}$	$\frac{6}{B}$	$\frac{7}{C}$	$\frac{8}{D}$	$\frac{9}{F}$	$\frac{10}{G}$
$\frac{11}{H}$	$\frac{12}{J}$	$\frac{13}{K}$	$\frac{14}{L}$	$\frac{15}{M}$	$\frac{16}{N}$	$\frac{17}{P}$	$\frac{18}{Q}$	$\frac{19}{R}$	$\frac{20}{S}$
$\frac{21}{T}$	$\frac{22}{V}$	$\frac{23}{W}$	$\frac{24}{Y}$						

REFORMATION DAY

43. MARTIN LUTHER'S COAT OF ARMS

October 31 is Reformation Day. It is a day all Christians remember Martin Luther, a German monk who left the Catholic church because he disagreed with some things the church taught. Luther loved the Bible and some of his favorite verses are used in his coat of arms.

Surely he has borne our griefs and carried our sorrows. Isa. 53:4

For God so loved the world that he gave his one and only Son. John 3:16

I am . . . the beginning and the ending. Rev. 1:8

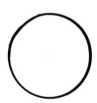

Look, the lamb of God, who takes away the sin of the world. John 1:29

Use these colors for the coat of arms: cross—black; heart—red; flower—white; inside of circle beyond flower—yellow.

44. 95 THESES

Color and cut out the text and paste it to the church door.

THANKSGIVING DAY

45. TRIANGLE MESSAGE

Here is a Thanksgiving Message for everyone. To discover what it is, start at the letter O and the arrow. Then skip over every other letter in two trips around the triangle. Print the letters on the blanks below the triangle to decipher the message.

_____

_____

_____

46. TURKEY ESCAPE

This turkey wants to escape to the woods before Thanksgiving Day. Can you help him find the right path?

47. SCRAMBLED PRAISES

Each of these drawings contains the letters in the name of something to be thankful for. How many can you unscramble?

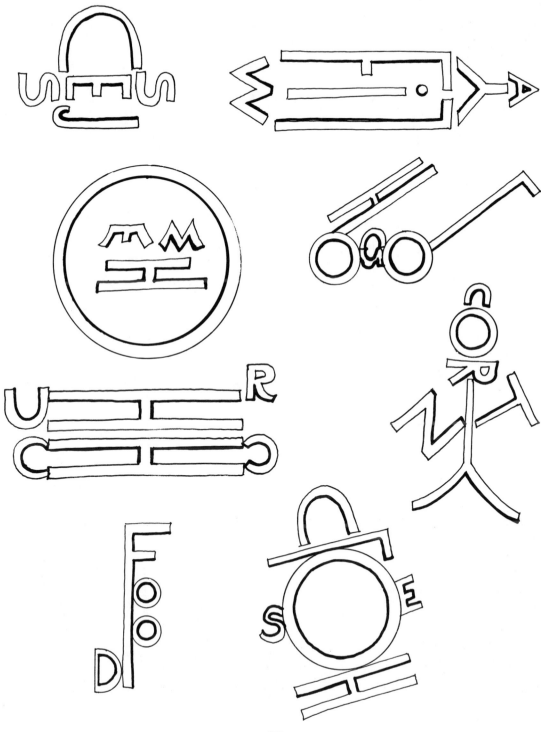

48. SMOKE SIGNALS

Can you read Joel's message? Follow the white smoke all the way up to a letter and then write the letter in one of the squares above the smoke.

T H T A P B N K S B W E S I O T I E O N I G N O J E D

ADVENT

49. MICAH'S MESSAGE

Many years before the birth of Christ, the prophet Micah made this prophecy. Can you read the message? If you need a clue turn the page upside down.

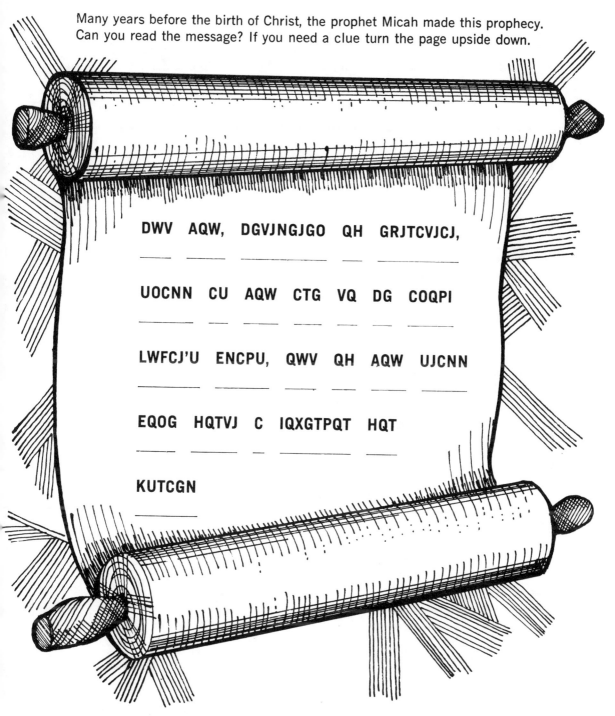

DWV AQW, DGVJNGJGO QH GRJTCVJCJ,

_____

UOCNN CU AQW CTG VQ DG COQPI

_____

LWFCJ'U ENCPU, QWV QH AQW UJCNN

_____

EQOG HQTVJ C IQXGTPQT HQT

_____

KUTCGN

_____

Take each letter and go backwards two letters from it in the alphabet.

50. ADVENT

The period including the four Sundays before Christmas is known as "advent." The word **advent** comes from two Latin words, **ad vento,** and means arrival, or coming toward. The advent season is a time for remembering the first time Jesus came to earth as a baby, and for reminding ourselves that He will come again to take all who love and trust in Him to be with Himself. Fill in the blanks below to make a word in the squares.

He announced the coming of Jesus.

     _ _ _ _

Jesus was born in the city of _____, called Bethlehem.

     _ _ _

Jesus is both God and Man; God is His father, and His mother was the _____ Mary.

     _ _ _ _ _

Isaiah foretold that one of Jesus' names would be "_____ Father."

     _ _ _ _ _ _ _ _

Jesus was born in a stable because there was _____ room for them in the inn.

     _

Caesar Augustus issued a decree that all the world should be _____.

     _ _ _ _

51. THE ADVENT WREATH

Some churches display an Advent Wreath during the advent season. It is made of evergreens (representing life) and has four candles in it. Three of the candles are purple, (representing royalty) and one candle is pink, or rose color. One of the purple candles is lit during the first week of advent, and another one is lit during each week that follows. The pink candle is lit on the third Sunday of advent, known as Gaudate Sunday. (Gaudate comes from the Latin word which means "rejoice.") Sometimes a white candle is placed in the center of the wreath to be lit on Christmas Eve.

Here is an Advent Wreath for you to color, following the directions given above. Perhaps you might like to make a real Advent Wreath for your family to use!

52. NAMES OF JESUS

The Bible uses many different names for Jesus. If you look up these verses, you will find the names with which to fill in the blanks. When you are all done, another of Jesus' names will appear in the vertical row of boxes.

Isaiah 53:3

Isaiah 9:6

Luke 2:11
(first name given)

Matthew 16:13

John 8:58

Revelation 15:3
(third name listed)

Revelation 4:8
(first name listed)

53. AN ADVENT CALENDAR TO MAKE

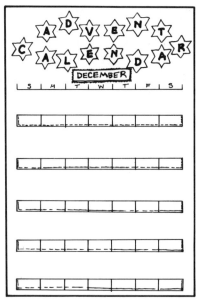

Count the days from December 1 until Christmas by adding a new picture each day.
Materials and Procedures for Making a Felt Calendar:
One piece of felt, 24″ x 36″
Five pieces of felt, 1″ x 18″
sewing machine, thread, magic marker
Lay strip of felt 3 inches from the bottom edge and 3 inches from each side edge of the large felt piece. Pin in place. Stitch ¼″ from the bottom and sides of the strip. Then stitch 2½″ from the side seam to form a pocket. Make 7 pockets on each strip. (Each will measure 2½″ wide.)
Measure 3 inches up from the top of the stitched-on felt piece and lay another strip. Repeat the sewing procedures.
Measure 3 inches up from the top of the second stitched-on felt piece and lay another strip. Repeat for remaining strips.

Materials and Procedures for Making a Poster Board Calendar:
One standard size poster board 22″ x 28″
Eighteen check-size envelopes
glue, scissors, magic marker
Seal the envelopes. Cut off each end of the envelope one inch from the edge. Use these ends as pockets, placing one row of seven pockets three inches up from the bottom edge of the poster board. Overlap edges of envelopes so they will fit on the board. Glue them in place. Repeat procedure for four more rows of pockets.

Use magic marker to write ADVENT CALENDAR, DECEMBER, and the days of the week above the seven columns. Cut out the 25 pictures on the next pages, color them, and mount them on construction paper. Put the picture marked "1" in whatever day the first day of December happens to fall on and continue filling in the calendar with one picture a day until Christmas.

THE ANGEL GABRIEL ANNOUNCED JESUS' COMING.

14 "HE HAS . . . A NAME WRITTEN, KING OF KINGS AND LORD OF LORDS

15 "JOY TO THE WORLD"

16

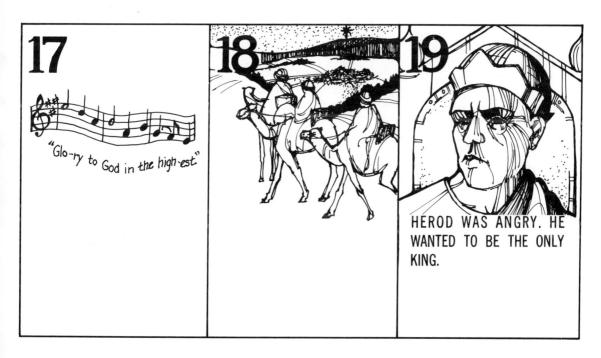

17 "Glo-ry to God in the high-est"

18

19 HEROD WAS ANGRY. HE WANTED TO BE THE ONLY KING.

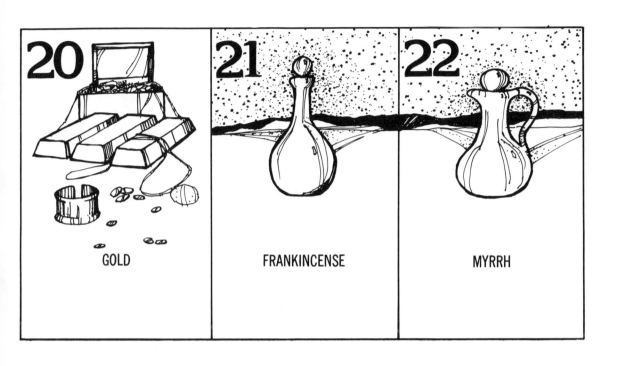

GOLD

FRANKINCENSE

MYRRH

COME AND WORSHIP

54. ADVENT CALENDAR

Many people use a special calendar to mark off the days from December 1 to Christmas. This is the time of year called Advent, which means to look forward to some important event or thing. Christians are looking forward to celebrating the birth of Christ.

The calendar on the next two pages has twenty-four different names of Jesus and also the spot in the Bible where that name is found.

Very carefully remove the sheets so that your calendar will not have any rips in it. Then paste the calendar to (red or green or whatever is your favorite color of construction paper). Punch two small holes near the top edge and insert string or yarn to hang it.

Each day read the passage and color in the square and date. Use bright colors.

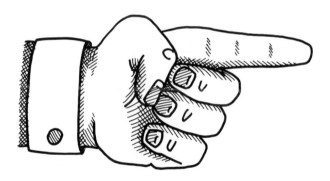

ADVENT CALENDAR

1 BRIGHT AND MORNING STAR Numbers 24:17	2 THE WAY TO GOD John 14:5-7	3 GOD'S MESSENGER John 8:42	4 BREAD OF LIFE John 6:32-58	5 FRIEND OF SINNERS Luke 5:27-32
6 GREAT DOCTOR John 5:1-9; Matthew 15:30	7 SON OF MAN Luke 22:69-70	8 LIVING WATER John 7:37	9 FRIEND OF CHILDREN Mark 10:13-16	10 THE DOOR John 10:9-11

11 THE TRUTH John 14:5-15	**12** TRUE VINE John 15:1-9	**13** SON OF DAVID Matthew 20:29-34
14 THE REDEEMER Titus 2:11-14	**15** TEACHER John 3:1-11	
16 STONE Luke 20:17; I Corinthians 10:4	**17** THE LAMB OF GOD John 1:29	**18** THE RESURRECTION AND THE LIFE John 11:21-27
19 ANOINTED ONE Luke 16:22	**20** THE LIGHT John 8:12-18	
21 GOOD SHEPHERD John 10:1-16	**22** PROPHET John 6:4; Deuteronomy 18:15	**23** THE KING John 7:12-15; Matthew 2:2
24 SON OF GOD Luke 3:21, 22	**25**	

CHRISTMAS

55. STAR PUZZLE

Each of the words which goes in this star puzzle begins with the letter "S" you see in the middle. One letter goes in each of the small circles.

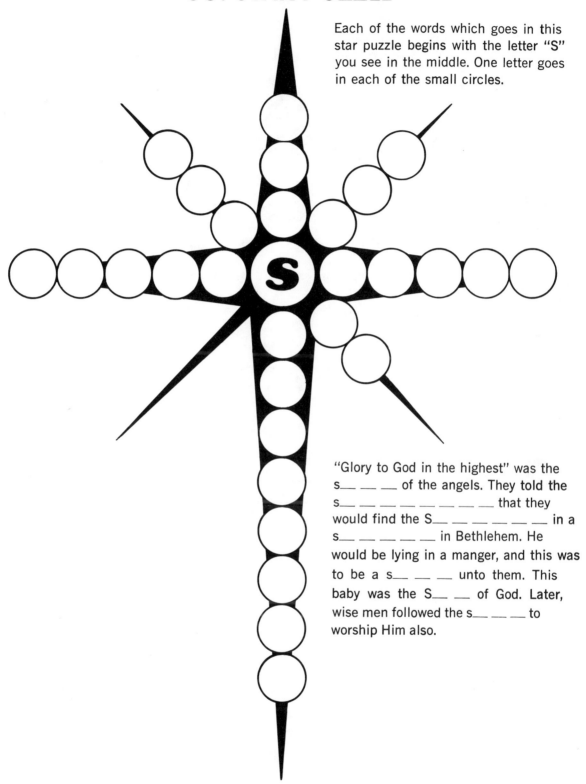

"Glory to God in the highest" was the s__ __ __ of the angels. They told the s__ __ __ __ __ __ __ __ that they would find the S__ __ __ __ __ __ in a s__ __ __ __ __ in Bethlehem. He would be lying in a manger, and this was to be a s__ __ __ unto them. This baby was the S__ __ of God. Later, wise men followed the s__ __ __ to worship Him also.

56. CHRISTMAS HIDE-AND-SEEK

Hidden in the puzzle below are many of the words that we often think of in connection with the Christmas story. The words might be spelled vertically, horizontally, or diagonally, and the spelling could start either at the top, or the bottom.

```
A  S  W  O  R  S  H  I  P  B  A  B  S  N
N  E  I  S  H  J  O  S  E  P  H  A  H  G
G  J  S  M  A  B  E  T  H  L  E  H  E  M
E  E  E  T  A  R  Y  A  R  R  D  E  P  H
L  S  M  S  A  N  G  B  L  O  A  R  H  S
S  H  E  A  U  R  G  L  R  I  V  U  E  O
M  A  N  R  R  S  H  E  U  V  I  A  R  N
G  N  N  A  R  Y  H  S  R  A  D  O  D  G
I  Y  U  M  E  R  H  J  O  S  Q  W  S  A
```

See how many of these words you can find:

ANGELS	HEROD
SHEPHERDS	DAVID
WISE MEN	BETHLEHEM
STAR	INN
MARY	MANGER
JOSEPH	WORSHIP
JESUS	SAVIOR
STABLE	SONG

57. SOME CHRISTMAS PEOPLE

Hidden in these pictures are the letters from the names of some people we read about in the Bible's Christmas story. How many names can you unscramble without looking at the answers?

58. CHRISTMAS GIFTS STACK-A-WORD

These are some of the "Christmas gifts" we receive by accepting the gift Jesus came to give us.

Discover what these gifts are by looking up the following verses:

ACROSS	DOWN
4. John 14:16	1. Matthew 11:29
7. John 10:10	2. Psalm 51:12
8. John 14:27	3. Isaiah 40:31
9. John 3:16	5. John 14:2
10. Isaiah 60:1a	6. Psalm 121:2

59. WHO SAID IT?

1. "Blessed art thou among women, and blessed is the fruit of thy womb." Luke 1:42 _____

2. "My soul doth magnify the Lord." Luke 1:46 _____

3. "In Bethlehem of Judea; for thus it is written by the prophet." Matthew 2:5 _____

4. "He shall be great, and shall be called the Son of the Highest." Luke 1:32 _____

5. "His name is John." Luke 1:63 _____

6. "Lord, now lettest thou thy servant depart in peace, according to thy word: For mine eyes have seen thy salvation." Luke 2:29-30 _____

7. "Where is he that is born King of the Jews?" Matthew 2:2 _____

8. "Glory to God in the highest, and on earth, peace." Luke 2:14 _____

9. "Go, and search diligently for the young child." Matthew 2:8 _____

10. "Let us now go even unto Bethlehem, and see this thing which is come to pass." Luke 2:15 _____

60. HELP THE WISE MEN FOLLOW THE STAR

61. MAKE-A-WORD

Can you make at least fifty words from the letters in

J O Y   T O   T H E   W O R L D ?

_____	_____	_____
_____	_____	_____
_____	_____	_____
_____	_____	_____
_____	_____	_____
_____	_____	_____
_____	_____	_____
_____	_____	_____
_____	_____	_____
_____	_____	_____
_____	_____	_____
_____	_____	_____
_____	_____	_____
_____	_____	_____
_____	_____	_____

62. WORD SQUARE

The words of the Christmas story have been hidden in the word square. If a word appears more than once in the story, it is hidden only once in the square. Look up, down, sideways, backwards, and diagonally to find the words. Many letters are used more than once.

AND THERE WERE IN THE SAME COUNTRY SHEPHERDS ABIDING IN THE FIELD, KEEPING WATCH OVER THEIR FLOCK BY NIGHT. AND, LO, THE ANGEL OF THE LORD CAME UPON THEM, AND THE GLORY OF THE LORD SHONE ROUND ABOUT THEM: AND THEY WERE SORE AFRAID. AND THE ANGEL SAID UNTO THEM, FEAR NOT: FOR, BEHOLD, I BRING YOU GOOD TIDINGS OF GREAT JOY, WHICH SHALL BE TO ALL PEOPLE. FOR UNTO YOU IS BORN THIS DAY IN THE CITY OF DAVID A SAVIOUR, WHICH IS CHRIST THE LORD.

C	E	T	A	M	S	A	J	A	Y	B	R	E	A	D	A	S
O	E	G	G	O	G	Y	F	S	K	I	N	E	A	Y	O	A
S	A	M	N	N	N	A	G	L	O	R	Y	U	Q	E	T	D
E	R	J	A	I	I	D	N	U	O	R	E	M	E	H	T	L
P	W	O	G	C	D	T	I	B	T	C	K	M	I	T	H	O
H	A	H	O	S	I	I	R	E	N	A	K	S	O	P	E	H
B	T	N	O	A	T	L	B	M	U	N	P	F	E	A	R	E
A	C	M	D	Y	K	O	N	A	D	G	T	O	G	F	E	B
B	H	G	B	R	E	R	O	S	H	E	P	H	E	R	D	S
C	I	T	Y	T	E	D	V	H	A	L	G	R	E	A	T	A
W	H	O	O	N	P	S	E	O	E	V	C	H	R	I	S	T
H	W	U	U	U	I	A	R	N	E	F	I	E	L	D	H	U
I	E	P	T	O	N	I	W	E	R	E	J	O	Y	R	A	O
C	R	O	R	C	G	D	A	V	I	D	S	U	U	D	L	B
H	E	N	F	O	R	R	T	H	A	T	H	E	I	R	L	A

63. HIDDEN OBJECTS

Can you find these things hidden in this drawing?

star	camel
shepherd	cross
lamb	the name JESUS
angel	

64. A MESSAGE FOR JOSEPH

After the birth of Jesus, an angel appeared to Joseph with a very important message. See if you can decode the message, using the key at the bottom of this page.

___ ___ ___ ___ ___ , ___ ___ ___ ___ ___ ___ ___
3 2 1 5 15   8 3 7 15   8 24 15

___ ___ ___ ___ ___ ___ ___ ___ ___ ___ ___ ___ ___
23 19 11 16 21   9 24 1 10 12   3 16 12

___ ___ ___ ___ ___ ___ ___ ___ ___ ___ ___ ___
24 1 5   13 19 8 24 15 2   3 16 12

___ ___ ___ ___ ___ ___ ___ ___ ___ ___ ___ ___ ___
18 10 15 15   1 16 8 19   15 21 23 22 8

1	2	3	4	5	6	7	8	9	10	11	12	13	14	15	16	17	18	19	20	21	22	23	24	25	26
I	R	A	J	S	B	K	T	C	L	U	D	M	V	E	N	W	F	O	X	G	P	Y	H	Q	Z

65. NAMES JESUS CALLED HIMSELF

66. UNFINISHED LETTERS

Mary, Joseph, Zacharias, and the shepherds all had a common experience. What was it? Parts of the capital letters in the boxes below were left out. You will find the missing parts in the bag. Use the missing parts to finish the letters and answer the question.

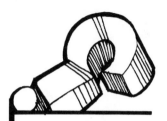

67. WHO AM I?

Give yourself 5 points if you can guess correctly with only the first clue; 3 points if you can guess on the second clue; and 1 point if you can guess after the third clue.

1. I am the priest whose speech was taken from him for a short time, as a sign from God.
   My wife's name was Elisabeth.
   My son became known as John the Baptist.
   Who am I? _____ Points: _____

2. I wanted to be the only king of the Jews.
   I was asked where to find the baby who was born to be the King of the Jews.
   I had all the young children in Bethlehem killed in my attempt to get rid of any other would-be king.
   Who am I? _____ Points: _____

3. I was a carpenter in Nazareth.
   An angel paid me an important visit.
   The mother of Jesus became my wife.
   Who am I? _____ Points: _____

4. All I usually had inside me was hay,
   Until the night when all the inns in Bethlehem were full.
   That night I held the baby Jesus.
   What am I? _____ Points: _____

5. We were warned by God in a dream to go home a different way.
   Herod asked us what time the star appeared.
   We brought gifts of gold, frankincense, and myrrh.
   Who are we? _____ Points: _____

6. I made a very important announcement without ever saying a word.
   Shepherds and kings received my message.
   You could have found me directly above the place where the child Jesus was.
   What am I? _____ Points: _____

Total Points: _____

68. TRUE OR FALSE?

If the statement is **true,** circle the letter in the True column. If the statement is **false,** circle the letter in the False column.

TRUE	FALSE	
4 **B**	2 **O**	Herod really wanted to worship Jesus.
4 **S**	2 **L**	When the angel had told Mary she was to be the mother of Jesus, she said, "How can this be?"
7 **S**	3 **R**	As a sign that God would do what He said, Zacharias was made deaf for a short time.
5 **H**	6 **M**	King David was Jesus' great-great-(many times great) grandfather.
5 **N**	7 **P**	The angel told Joseph to leave Bethlehem and take his family back to Nazareth.
6 **I**	1 **E**	Anna was an old woman who lived in the temple. She gave thanks to God when she saw the baby Jesus.
1 **W**	3 **A**	The Wise men presented gifts to Jesus.

Now put the letters you circled in the squares below, matching the number of the square with the number beside the letter.

1	2	3	4	5	6	7

Shepherds, then later the Wise men came to Jesus to do this—and we can do it, too.

69. WHAT DID JESUS COME TO BRING?

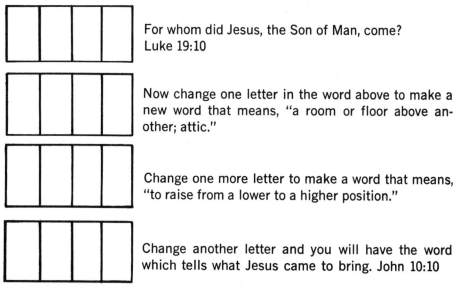

For whom did Jesus, the Son of Man, come? Luke 19:10

Now change one letter in the word above to make a new word that means, "a room or floor above another; attic."

Change one more letter to make a word that means, "to raise from a lower to a higher position."

Change another letter and you will have the word which tells what Jesus came to bring. John 10:10

CHANGE THE LETTERS

70. MARY'S SONG

Hidden in the puzzle below are words from the first part of the happy song Mary sang about being the mother of Jesus. It is found in Luke 1:46 and 47.

My soul doth magnify the Lord.
And my spirit hath rejoiced in God my Saviour.

```
M Y O D S L O H
S A V I O U R T
M N G A U T I A
Y D G N L R H H
R E J O I C E D
L E R P D F H M
U D S E H T Y O
```

71. BELL MAZE

72. CHRISTMAS MOBILE

You can make a very special Christmas mobile by coloring the fronts and backs of these figures. Cut them out and paste together. Punch out a small hole and put a piece of string through each. Put a knot at the end so that the string cannot slip through the hole. Bend a lightweight coat hanger and hang the figures from it.

73. A REBUS PUZZLE

Write the letters of the picture clues and then add or subtract letters, following the math signs.

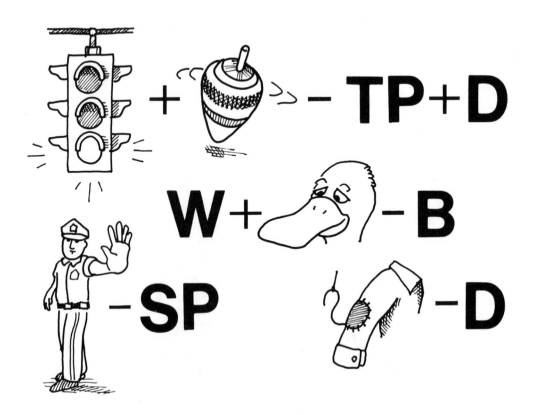

74. TRUE OR FALSE

T F

Color the star under the T or F column, depending on whether the statement is true or false.

1 The shepherds were watching sheep on the hillside near Bethany.

2 The name of Jesus' mother was Mary.

3 Jesus' father, Joseph, was a fisherman.

4 When Jesus was only a young baby, his parents took him to Syria.

5 Jesus grew up in the city of Nazarene.

6 Anna and Simeon were waiting for Jesus in the Temple.

7 Ananias was an old priest who was told he would not see death until he would see Jesus.

8 John the Baptist was a nephew of Jesus.

9 Jesus was born in the city of Bethlehem.

10 Some wisemen from the West brought gifts to Jesus.

75. NAMES OF JESUS

All the names of Jesus listed below fit into this puzzle, one letter to a square.

KING   CHRIST   SAVIOR   MESSIAH
LAMB   MASTER   TEACHER
LORD

76. BLESSED CHRISTMAS

Using only the letters in BLESSED CHRISTMAS, see how many words you can make.

_____

_____

_____

_____

_____

_____

_____

77. MESSAGES FROM ANGELS

Fit one letter in each column into a square above the column. A colored square means the end of a word. When you have solved the puzzle, read across the squares.

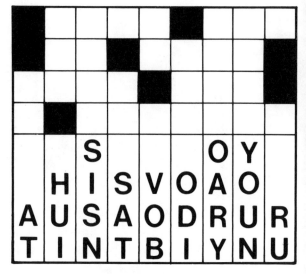

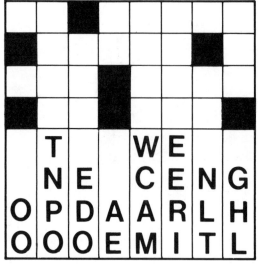

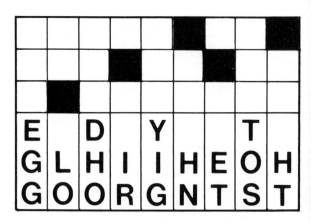

78. HIDDEN OBJECTS

Can you find a shepherd, four sheep, two angels, three stars, a crown, and a cross in the puzzle below?

79. A DOT-TO-DOT DRAWING

Beginning at #1, draw a line from one dot to the next and you will discover an animal that walked a long way carrying someone who wanted to see Jesus.

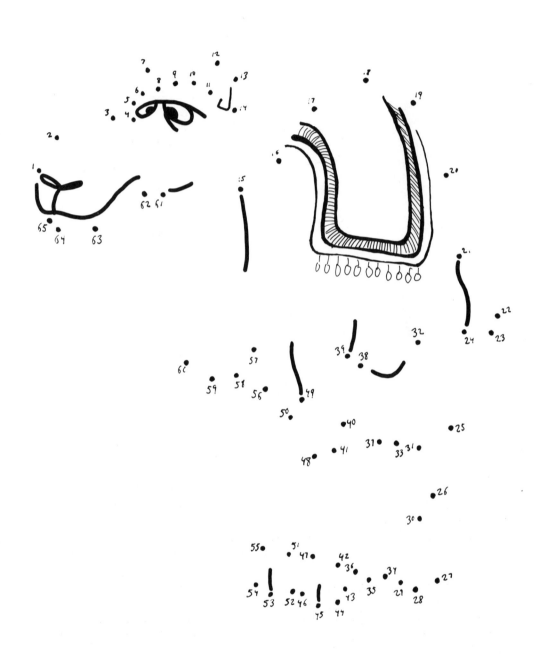

80. A CHRISTMAS STAR

This is a Christmas star because if you fill in the numbers correctly, the sum of the four numbers in any direction will total 25. Another clue is that only the numbers from 2 to 11 are used, and two numbers are used twice.

If you need more help, fill in the blanks first so you will know exactly where to place each number.

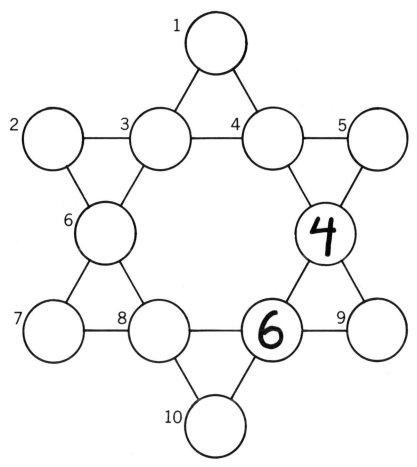

1 How many days old was Jesus when He was named? Luke 2:21
2 At what hour did the nobleman's son become well? John 4:52
3 How many lepers were healed? Luke 17:17
4 How many coins did the widow give? Mark 12:42
5 How many filled waterpots did Jesus turn into wine at the wedding in Cana? John 2:6
6 How many days was Lazarus in the grave? John 11:17
7 How many times did Peter deny Jesus? Mark 14:15
8 How many loaves of bread did the young boy have in his lunch? Luke 9:13
9 To how many disciples did Jesus appear as they gathered on the night of His resurrection? Mark 16:14
10 How many lepers did not come back to thank Jesus? Luke 17:17

81. SILENT NIGHT

Hidden in the puzzle below are the words from the old Christmas carol:

Silent night, holy night,
All is calm, All is bright,
'Round yon virgin mother and child.
Holy infant, so tender and mild,
Sleep in heavenly peace.

```
M A R D E S D A N T
F O R D R O U N D N
Y E T A N T O D L A
L E H O H A Y S I F
N V G G L C A L M N
E S I L E N T J O I
V N N R E D N E T H
A S T H G I R B H O
E L I C H I L D E N
H O L Y O N N I R P
S L E E P E A C E R
```

82. A DOT-TO-DOT DRAWING

Beginning at #1, draw a line from one dot to the next and you will discover what Joseph and Mary took with them to the temple when Jesus was presented to the Lord.

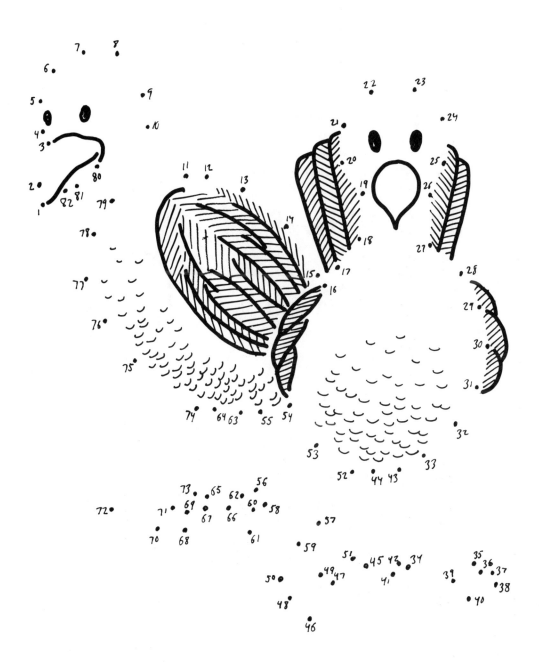

83. CHRISTMAS TREE SYMBOLS

You can make some very special decorations for your Christmas tree by coloring and cutting out these symbols for Christ. Often the symbols are made in gold and white but you can choose any color you like. Be sure to read about the symbol so you will know what it means.

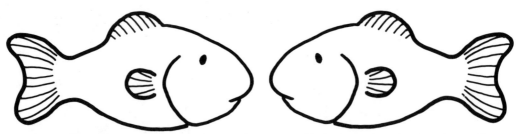

Soon after Jesus went back to heaven, Christians used the sign of a fish as a secret way to show they believed in Christ.

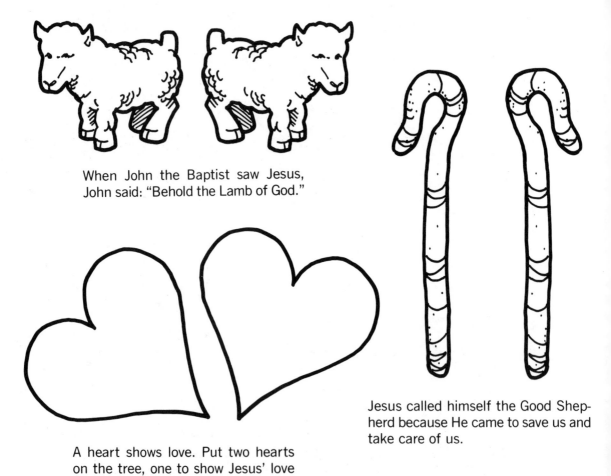

When John the Baptist saw Jesus, John said: "Behold the Lamb of God."

Jesus called himself the Good Shepherd because He came to save us and take care of us.

A heart shows love. Put two hearts on the tree, one to show Jesus' love to you and one to show your love to Jesus.

The star reminds us of the star that guided the wisemen to Bethlehem.

A candle reminds us that Jesus said He was the light of the world.

The cross could stand for Jesus' suffering or it could remind us of Jesus' love.

Jesus is a king over every king who ever lived.

When the letters P and X are used together like this, they are a monogram for Christ. This is a very old symbol. The letter P is actually a Greek letter called *rho* and the letter X is called *chi* in Greek. Now we call these two letters *ChiRho*.

84. FIND THE MESSAGE

Skip every other letter to find a hidden message about Mary's baby. A star marks the beginning of a new word. Color the squares of the letters you use red. Color the other squares green.

▶	H	O	E	H
*	W	E	A	T
S	G	*	N	D
A	I	M	L	E
N	D	O	*	J
D	E	T	S	R
U	C	S	A	!

85. MAZE

This wiseman noticed that two bells were missing from his camel's bridle. Can you help him find both bells?

149

86. SNOWFLAKES

Trace around a cup on a plain piece of paper. Or use this pattern to practice.

1 Fold circle in half.
2 Divide half circle into thirds.
3 Fold right third up.
4 Fold left third down.
5 Cut notches in sides and top to form design.
6 Carefully unfold.
7 Hang with white thread from Christmas tree branches or attach to a window or mirror.

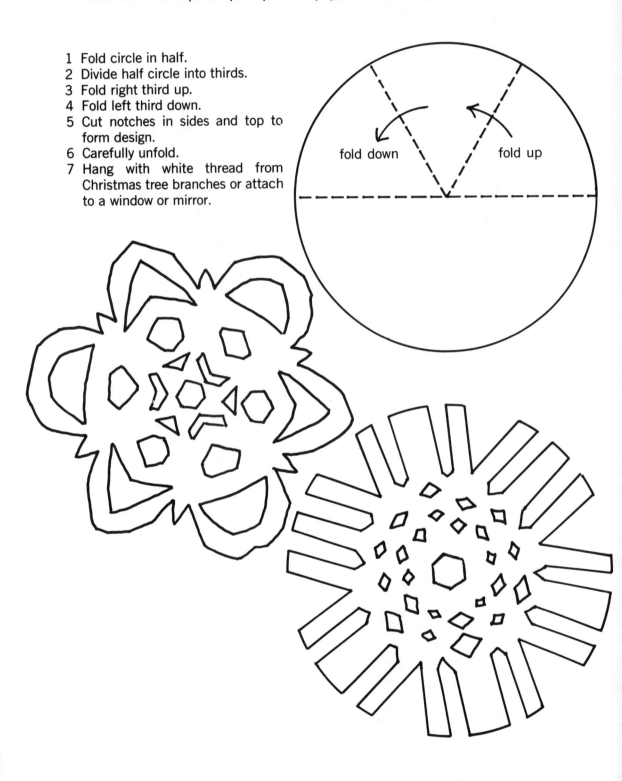

fold down   fold up

87. BOOKMARKS

Color the bookmarks. Cut them out and paste each one on a piece of colored paper that is about a half inch wider and longer than the bookmark.

88. COLOR BY NUMBER

Color the picture below, using the following colors: Spaces marked 1—blue; 2—green; 3—red; 4—light brown; 5—yellow; blank spaces, leave white.

89. STAR MAZE

See if you can start at one point of the star and work your way out of the maze.

90. FIND THE HIDDEN STARS

There are fifteen stars hidden in this drawing. How many can you find?

ANSWERS

2. THEY KNEW JESUS

1-1
2-4
3-6
4-5
5-2
6-3

3. GOOD SHEPHERD STACK-A-WORD

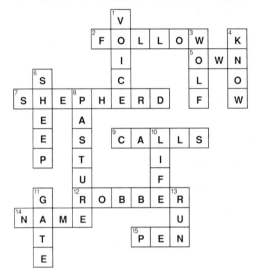

4. SMOKE SIGNALS

Glory to God

6. JESUS' WORDS

I am the good shepherd.
The good shepherd lays down
his life for the sheep.

9. SMOKE SIGNALS

God loves you.

10. SIX LOVE MESSAGES

1

W	H	O			S	H	A	L	L
	S	E	P	A	R	A	T	E	
	U	S		F	R	O	M		
T	H	E		L	O	V	E		
O	F		C	H	R	I	S	T	

2

A	S		T	H	E		F	
A	T	H	E	R		H	A	
T	H		L	O	V	E	D	
	M	E		S	O		H	
A	V	E		I		L	O	
V	E	D		Y	O	U		

3

T	H	O	U		S	H	A	L	T
	L	O	V	E		T	H	Y	
N	E	I	G	H	B	O	R		A
S		T	H	Y	S	E	L	F	

4

	F	O	R		T	H	I	S	
I	S		T	H	E		L	O	V
E		O	F		G	O	D		T
H	A	T		W	E		K	E	E
P		H	I	S		C	O	M	M
A	N	D	M	E	N	T	S		

5

	I	F		G	O	D		S
O		L	O	V	E	D		U
S		W	E		O	U	G	H
T		A	L	S	O		T	O
	L	O	V	E		O	N	E
	A	N	O	T	H	E	R	

155

6

I	F			Y	E		L
O	V	E			M	E	
K	E	E	P			M	Y
	C	O	M	M	A	N	
D	M	E	N	T	S		

12. WHY?

Because he loves me.

15. EASTER WORD HUNT

16. RESURRECTION STACK-A-WORD

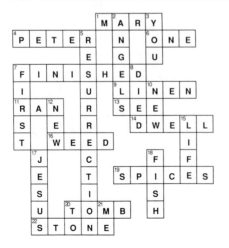

17. WHICH ARE EASTER PICTURES?

All of the pictures relate to the Easter story.

18. FOLLOW THE EASTER STORY

Resurrection

20. GOD'S EASTER GIFT

For God so loved the world that he gave his one and only Son, that whoever believes in him shall not perish but have eternal life.

21. WHO AM I?

1. angel
2. Joseph of Arimathea
3. guards at Jesus' tomb
4. Mary Magdalene, the other Mary, and other women
5. centurion

22. SOME EASTER PEOPLE

1. Caiaphas
2. Pilate
3. Herod
4. Simon
5. Jesus
6. Peter

23. CHANGE-A-LETTER

I serve the risen Jesus.

24. TRUE OR FALSE

False
True
True
False
True
False

25. EASTER V.I.P. STACK-A-WORD

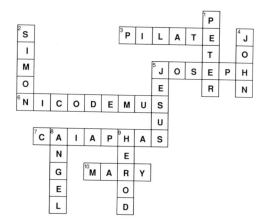

26. WHO SAID IT?

1. Jesus
2. Pilate's wife
3. Jesus
4. Peter
5. Pilate
6. Judas
7. Jesus

8. the high priest
9. the Jews
10. the centurion
11. Jesus
12. Jesus
13. Mary of Magdala
14. the angel

27. PICTURE MESSAGE

God's Word—Good News

28. A WALL OF LETTERS

Thy word is a lamp to my feet and a light to my path. Ps. 119:105

29. ASCENSION WORD FIND

nail(s)	lain
snail(s)	sail(ed)
snare(d)	alas
send(s)	easel(s)
lend(s)	ease(d)
den(s)	seal
all	secede(d)
call(ed, s)	ale(s)
fall(s)	sale
cell(s)	dean
sell(s)	lean
ascend(ed)	clean(ed, s)
sane	sled(s)
lane(s)	slide(s)
cane(s)	

32. WORD SEARCH

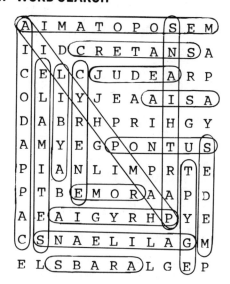

34. CIRCLE MESSAGE

They were filled with the Holy Spirit.

35. A WALL OF LETTERS

The grace of the Lord Jesus Christ
and the love of God
and the fellowship of the Holy Spirit
be with you all. 2 Cor. 13:14

37. A FAMOUS MOTHER

Mary

39. MOTHER'S DAY CODED MESSAGE

Her children arise up, and call her blessed; her husband also and he praiseth her. Prov. 31:38

40. THE FIRST FATHER

Adam

42. FATHER'S DAY CODED MESSAGE

Hear the instruction of thy father. Prov. 1:8

45. TRIANGLE MESSAGE

O give thanks to the Lord for he is good.

47. SCRAMBLED PRAISES

Jesus	family
home	school
church	food
clothes	country

48. SMOKE SIGNALS

Thanks be to God.

49. MICAH'S MESSAGE

But you, Bethlehem of Ephrathah, small as you are to be among Judah's class, out of you shall come forth a governor for Israel.

50. ADVENT

A NGEL
D AVID
V IRGIN
E VERLASTING
N O
T AXED

52. NAMES OF JESUS

M AN OF SORROWS
E VERLASTING FATHER
S AVIOUR
S ON OF MAN
I AM
A LMIGHTY
H OLY

55. STAR PUZZLE

56. CHRISTMAS HIDE-AND-SEEK

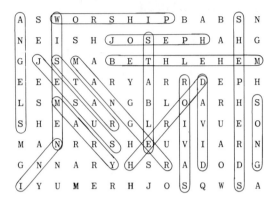

57. SOME CHRISTMAS PEOPLE

1—Jesus; 2—Herod; 3—Wise men; 4—Shepherds; 5—Gabriel; 6—Joseph.

58. CHRISTMAS GIFTS STACK-A-WORD

Y   J   S
COMFORTER
P K Y R H
LIFE   PEACE
A   N   LOVE
C   G   P
E   LIGHT
H

59. WHO SAID IT?

1—Elisabeth; 2—Mary; 3—chief priests and scribes; 4—angel; 5—Zacharias; 6—Simeon; 7—Wise men; 8—a multitude of the heavenly hosts; 9—Herod; 10—Shepherds.

61. MAKE A WORD

		ROT	ODOR
WE	OR	DOOR	RODE
LO	WORD	HERD	LOWER
LED	ODE	OTTER	WHORL
TOE	OW	HERO	WOOD
HOW	TRY	RYE	WROTE
LEWD	WOOL	DO	OWL
DOT	LORE	RED	WHY
ORE	YE	WOE	HOOD
DOER	HOE	LOW	LOT
TOW	ROW	DEW	HO
HEW	JEW	JET	WED
JOT	YET	OTHER	DOE

62. WORD SQUARE

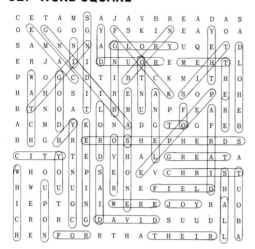

64. A MESSAGE FOR JOSEPH

Arise, take the young child and his mother and flee into Egypt.

65. NAMES JESUS CALLED HIMSELF

1—Light; 2—Truth; 3—Bread; 4—Life; 5—Door; 6—Alpha; 7—Omega; 8—Resurrection.

66. UNFINISHED LETTERS

An angel visit.

67. WHO AM I?

1—Zacharias; 2—Herod; 3—Joseph; 4—Manger; 5—Wise men; 6—Star.

68. TRUE OR FALSE?

A—O; B—S; C—R; D—H; E—P; F—I; G—W. WORSHIP.

69. WHAT DID JESUS COME TO BRING?

LOST
LOFT
LIFT
LIFE

70. MARY'S SONG

73. A REBUS PUZZLE

Peace on earth.
Good will to men.

74. TRUE OR FALSE

1. False, Bethlehem
2. True
3. False, carpenter
4. False, Egypt
5. False, Nazareth
6. True
7. False, Simeon
8. False, second cousin
9. True
10. False, East

75. NAMES OF JESUS

76. BLESSED CHRISTMAS

led	stem	lair
crib	met	air
star	mad	stair
mass	ate	rib
tree	eat	bad
his	meat	mess
mist	seat	miss
tire	tread	read
less	sled	sear
bled	the	ear
smash	cheer	mar
hair	heed	chair
air	rail	mail
sail	less	bless
slam	lamb	tame

77. MESSAGES FROM ANGELS

Unto you is born this day a saviour.
On earth peace, good will to men.
Glory to God in the highest.

80. A CHRISTMAS STAR

1—8
2—7
3—10
4—2
5—6
6—4
7—3
8—5
9—11
10—9

81. SILENT NIGHT

84. FIND THE MESSAGE

He was named Jesus.